CUSTOMER RELATIONSHIP MANAGEMENT

A powerful tool for attracting and retaining customers

Written by Antoine Delers
In collaboration with Anne-Christine Cadiat
Translated by Rebecca Neal

CUSTOMER RELATIONSHIP MANAGEMENT 1

Definition of the model

THEORY 4

The origins of CRM

Implementing a CRM strategy within a company

Understanding and adding value to the customer relationship

The advantages of CRM

EFFECTIVE MANAGEMENT OF CUSTOMER RELATIONSHIPS 16

A step-by-step guide

Recommendations

Case study

LIMITATIONS AND EXTENSIONS 30

Limitations and criticisms

Related models and extensions

SUMMARY 34

FURTHER READING 37

CUSTOMER RELATIONSHIP MANAGEMENT

- **Name:** customer relationship management (CRM).
- **Uses:** CRM is used in businesses and aims to optimise customer service, develop the sales force and provide statistical and customer monitoring tools for the purpose of marketing and data management.
- **Why is it successful?** CRM allows companies to improve the quality of customer relationships, personalise their offers, monitor relationships, identify opportunities and implement multichannel communication while reducing their effort (in spite of the large number of clients and prospects to manage) and guaranteeing the transmission of client knowledge within the organisation.
- **Key words:**
  - Attrition: the loss of customers over a given period, measured through the attrition rate; the opposite of retention, which corresponds to the rate of clients conserved over a given period.
  - Customer lifetime value: a prediction of the net profit value expected from a client throughout the entire duration of their relationship with the company.
  - Customer segmentation: the division and classification of customers into homogenous, distinct, profitable and reachable groups.
  - Data mining: all the statistical analysis tools and practices that use data, in particular customer data, to find significant information that can be used to develop marketing campaigns and other activities.

- Front office: unlike the back office, which is not visible to customers, the front office encompasses all the human and material resources in direct contact with the client.
- Key performances indicators (KPIs): key performance indicators are used by management and provide indications about performance and efficiency which measure the results of an activity such as, for example, a marketing campaign.
- Loyalty marketing: all the actions needed to stimulate and maintain customer relationships.
- Multichannel: the use of several means of communication between the company and the client, such as direct sales, phone, internet (social media, email, chat programmes, the company website and contact forms), and so on.
- One-to-one marketing: a type of marketing which contrasts with mass marketing in that it tries to communicate with each client separately to offer them a personalised service.
- Prospecting: the search for potential customers ("prospects") with the aim of turning them into consumers of the goods or service offered.

According to the English entrepreneur and iconic founder of Virgin Group Richard Branson (born in 1950), there are two keys to success: hiring talented people and listening carefully to the customer. This guide will focus on the second of these two vital points.

DEFINITION OF THE MODEL

Customer relationship management, or CRM, refers to all the strategies, tools and techniques that allow companies to track, manage and enrich their relationships with customers (including both current customers and former customers to win back) and prospects.

CRM software has now become virtually indispensable in most large companies. It allows businesses to keep a reliable and precise record of all the exchanges between the company and the customer, which allows them to personalise interactions in an attempt to win customer loyalty, or between the company and the prospect, thanks to integrated segmentation tools. Finally, it can be used in business reporting to produce general statistics and other important figures (such as key performance indicators.

An interesting thing about CRM is that it is traditionally seen as a front-office rather than a back-office tool. Front office, which is used in economic jargon to refer to the visible part of the iceberg, represents the part of the company that customers are aware of: salespeople, sales representatives, cashiers, ticket sellers, and so on. The back office encompasses all the tools and material and human resources of a company that the customers are not directly aware of, such as the accounting and finance departments.

THEORY

THE ORIGINS OF CRM

The origin of customer relationships goes back centuries: as soon as our ancestors had to prospect, sell items or provide an after-sales service, they were using this concept, although they did not define it as we do today. It was not until the development of information and communications technology in the 1990s that CRM was defined, and it was not applied strategically until the 2000s, when CRM software began to be used in businesses. Increasing competition, rising costs of prospecting in relation to the costs linked to creating customer loyalty and vast client bases because of the rise of consumerism are among the elements which encouraged the development of customer relationship management.

IMPLEMENTING A CRM STRATEGY WITHIN A COMPANY

Customer relationship management covers all the tools and techniques used in companies to manage their customer base by offering them a personalised service. In this way, the company can personally address each client, provided that they are identified in the system and assigned to a particular segment. The CRM approach optimises a company's customer service and sales force though statistical and client monitoring tools used for the purpose of management and marketing.

But how can you go about implementing a CRM strategy?

Provided you have the time and resources you need, anything is possible!

Implementing CRM

1. Optimisation of data:
   cleaning, reporting

2. Adapted technology:
   a system that is ergonomic and accessible to everyone
   (different profiles depending on the employees)

3. Process established:
   development of a workflow and strategies

4. Training and adaptation of workers:
   through suitable management

IN PRACTICE: CRM AS AN IT TOOL

It now seems obvious that an effective CRM strategy (automising the segmentation process, prospecting, creating customer loyalty, analysing customers, and so on) requires the use of CRM software. This can be a software application that is accessed from company computers, but also eCRM (CRM online) or mobile CRM (which is adapted for tablets and smartphones).

At present, there are a range of CRM solutions on the market from different IT providers, in particular Microsoft (Microsoft Dynamics CRM), SAP (SAP CRM) and Oracle (Oracle CRM). These applications are often linked to the company's enterprise resource planning

(EPR) and offer a unique and complete database, since they combine commercial, financial and logistical data, among others.

ERP

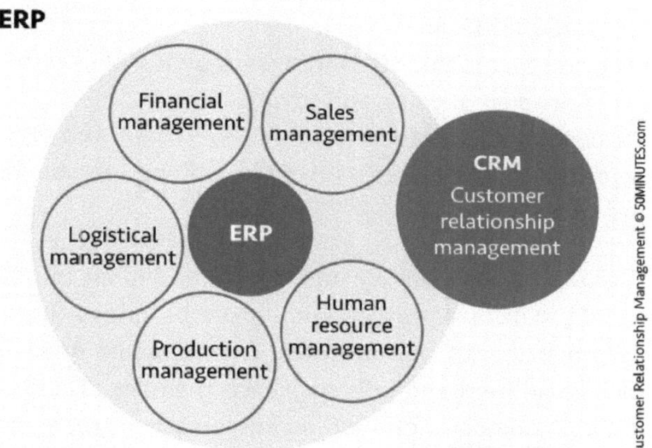

UNDERSTANDING AND ADDING VALUE TO THE CUSTOMER RELATIONSHIP

Segmentation and prospecting

Customer segmentation allows companies to organise existing or prospective clients into distinct homogenous groups, which can then be targeted with an effective, tailored message. Consumers in the same segment must have shared characteristics. Depending on whether the customer base is B2B (business to business) or B2C (business to consumer), certain types of criteria can be used when carrying out the segmentation:

- geographical variables (country, region or town),
- firmographic variables (industry, turnover, number of employees, and so on),
- sociodemographic variables (age, sex, number of children, stage of life, and so on),
- behavioural variables (advantages sought, shops visited, use of product, loyalty, and so on),
- socioeconomic variables (profession, income, and so on),
- psychographic variables (lifestyle, values, personality, and so on).

Each group must be unique and cannot be similar to other segments; in other words, you should not be able to confuse the segments with one another. The company needs to be able to address and influence each member of a group through a unique mode of communication (such as a marketing campaign). The segment must be large enough to be profitable and to justify a specific strategic approach. Finally, it must be possible to measure and operationalise it, because it is important to be able to determine the number of clients within each segment and to attribute a specific client type to a given segment based on predefined criteria.

Once the segmentation has been carried out, it is time for targeting and prospecting. Depending on the situation, there will be more or fewer groups of consumers segments; obviously, it is not helpful to focus on every group that has been defined. Segmentation allows companies to separate groups of potential customers on one hand, and groups of people who will probably never become customers on the other hand. Choosing to focus on one segment of consumers is known as targeting. The more precise the targeting, the most effective the prospecting phase will be.

Creating customer loyalty

The second approach in customer relationship management involves securing the loyalty of customers. It is often claimed that ensuring one client's loyalty is five times cheaper than attracting new customers. Consequently, it is in a company's best interests to lavish attention on its most important customers. Creating customer loyalty brings companies the complementary benefits of increasing their profits and establishing their position on the market.

The creation of customer loyalty can be explained through the following cycle: once the first contact between the company and the customer has been established, a sale can be made. If this happens, this is the precise moment that the customer becomes a "customer" and starts to form an opinion on their relationship with the seller. This is followed by the actual use of the product or the experience of the service, and the after-sales service which encompasses all the operations to resolve problems encountered by clients, the suggestion of new products, and so on. Customer satisfaction should therefore be at the centre of the company's concerns throughout the process of creating loyalty in order to establish a sales cycle.

Creation of loyalty

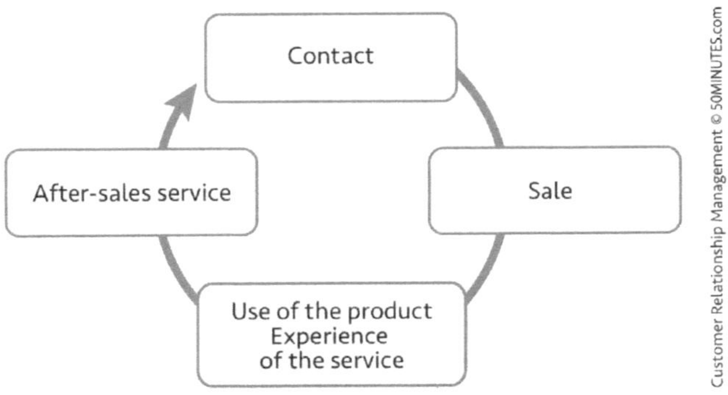

Finally, it is essential to measure and be aware of customer loyalty. Although there is no rate directly linked to this, you can get a good estimate by analysing some KPIs. These include the retention rate (the number of clients retained in relation to all the clients acquired over the course of a year) and the Net Promotor Score (NPS), which summarises the marks (from 1 to 10) given to companies by their customers. Companies with a score of 0 to 6 are called Detractors, those with a score of 7 to 8 are referred to as Passives and those with a score of 9 to 10 are known as Promoters. As well as these quantitative approaches, customer loyalty can also be calculated qualitatively. However, the results obtained are less precise and more difficult to compare.

Business reporting

The third and final approach to customer relationship management is statistical. CRM tools allow companies to exploit customer data in order to get KPIs from it and calculate different statistics related to marketing campaigns, product sales, and so on. The key indicators include:

- **The response rate**, meaning the number of people who responded to the company's sales offer. It can be calculated through a reply coupon used by the customer or through a promotional code encoded in a system.
- **The conversion rate**, meaning the number of prospects who become customers over a given period.
- **The retention rate**, meaning the number of customers retained over a given period in relation to the new clients converted over the same period. It contrasts with the attrition rate, which measures the number of clients lost.
- **The satisfaction rate**, which measures existing customers' satisfaction and can be complemented by the NPS.
- **The rate of complaints per customer**, which refers to the number of complaints recorded over a set period of time in relation to the overall client base.
- **Return on investment (ROI)**, meaning the income generated following a marketing campaign or the launch of a new product.
- **The cost of acquisition of a new client**, meaning the cost represented by the conversion and therefore the acquisition of a new client. It can be calculated in particular using the budget invested in a marketing campaign.
- **The net present value of the client**, meaning the present value of the future profits that a company can expect per client.

Good customer relationship management goes hand in hand with the effective use of data mining, which encompasses all the tools and techniques that can be used to extract significant data, including the correlations between the variables outlined previously. For example, this approach is favoured by credit agencies, who use it for credit scoring, meaning the calculation of the risk associated with a client who wants to borrow.

Credit scoring

In reality, this practice is based on the empirical study of loans already granted by the agency. By examining the rate of reimbursement of credit in relation to the characteristics of former recipients of loans (in particular their salary), which the new credit applicants also have, the banking agency is able to interpret the data it has at its disposal. This allows it to anticipate as well as possible the risk that new applicants will be unable to pay back their loans.

Data mining is also very useful for extracting consumption patterns. The aim here is to determine which products to suggest to a particular household based on their buying behaviour. As such, some chain stores use customers' loyalty cards to find out about their habits and suggest products adapted to their preferences. For example, a customer who loves sweets and chocolate will receive a catalogue with a special offer on chocolate bars on the front page, while their neighbour, who buys a lot of vegetables, will receive a limited time offer on courgettes and potatoes. In reality, they both belong to particular segments and communication is adapted depending on the group to better target their needs. By managing client data effectively, supermarket chains can put together a series of brochures based on the preferences of their different segments and use them to send out personalised offers.

While analysing its customers' shopping baskets, a large American company reportedly discovered a strong correlation between packs of beer and nappies. It would seem that on Saturdays mothers tended to stay home to look after their young children while fathers went out to buy nappies and took the opportunity to buy beer to drink that night. Having noticed this buying behaviour, the supermarket chain then decided to put nappies on the same shelf as beer. The company saw this sales strategy based on data mining as an easy way of increasing its sales.

THE ADVANTAGES OF CRM

The use of CRM tools offers many advantages. The main benefits are outlined below.

The centralisation and diffusion of client data within the company

- CRM allows companies to focus on relationships (B2B or B2C) and keep a record of exchanges with customers or suppliers. Furthermore, by making CRM accessible to everyone within the company, every employee, from the sales department to the invoicing service, can access this data more easily.
- It allows companies to optimise and structure the management of a very large number of customers, former customers and prospects, while continuing to offer a personalised service based on the segments defined through data analysis. Without a tool like this, unless the company knows each client personally, it is impossible to address their various customers as though they were unique.

The optimisation of the customer life cycle – between acquisition and the creation of loyalty

- CRM also allows the passive monitoring of customer value. If a customer has not bought anything for a set period of time, an alert can be triggered so that a salesperson deals with the situation and tries to win back their custom. This system ensures the continuity of the service. The aim is to bring as many customers as possible into the purchase loop.
- It makes it easier to anticipate customers' needs and expectations. By observing the client cycle, the company may be able to identify opportunities for cross-selling (the sale of a product from another category) and up-sel-

ling (the sale of an additional or more expensive product from the same category).

A win-win relationship thanks to personalised offers

- By analysing the data contained in the CRM system, companies can gain a better understanding of their customers' needs and buying behaviours, which allows them to adapt their offer (of products, including the distribution channel and targeted communication). In this way, it can increase performance as clients appreciate the personalised service, which will motivate them to keep buying from the company.

The advantages of CRM

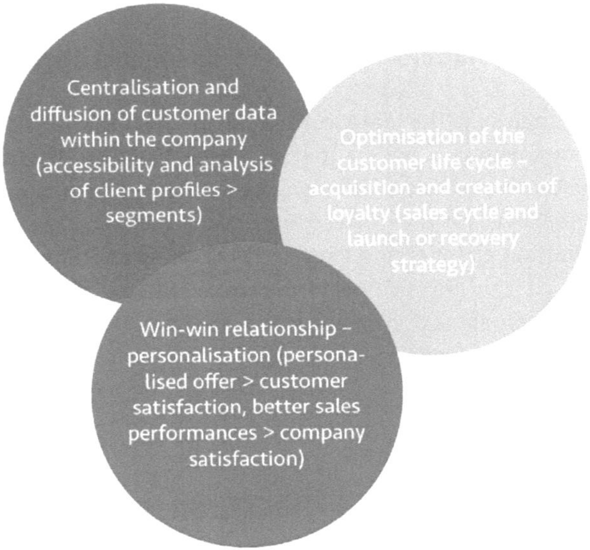

Centralisation and diffusion of customer data within the company (accessibility and analysis of client profiles > segments)

Optimisation of the customer life cycle – acquisition and creation of loyalty (sales cycle and launch or recovery strategy)

Win-win relationship – personalisation (personalised offer > customer satisfaction, better sales performances > company satisfaction)

EFFECTIVE MANAGEMENT OF CUSTOMER RELATIONSHIPS

A STEP-BY-STEP GUIDE

Step 1: Customer segmentation

Companies divide their customer base into different groups or segments in order to organise their strategy as effectively as possible. There are various ways of doing this, some of which are outlined below.

- **RFM (Recency, Frequency, Monetary Value) segmentation** divides customers into groups based on their buying habits over a given period.
  - When was their last purchase?
  - How often do they purchase?
  - How much do they spend?

  This method establishes a hierarchy of customers based on the value of their purchases; the biggest spenders should be prioritised and given the most attention, while those who spend less should be monitored and encouraged to spend more in order to move into a higher category. It may be worth getting back in touch with former customers to try and win them back.
- **Geographic segmentation** marks out a geographical zone (in the case of a shop, this is known as the catchment area) which contains every potential customer. This can be done by studying existing customers, for example by using postcodes, in order to see where most of them

come from. The company can then find new customers by concentrating its efforts on this area.

- **Segmentation based on the Pareto ratio**. According to the Pareto principle, 20% of a company's customers generate 80% of its revenue, so, as with RFM segmentation, it is a good idea to apply adapted strategies to each segmented group depending on the need to establish customer loyalty.

WHAT IS THE PARETO PRINCIPLE?

The Pareto principle, also known as the 80/20 rule, is a principle of analysis set out by the Italian economist Vilfredo Pareto (1848-1923). It states that 80% of effects come from 20% of causes. This ratio can be observed to a great or lesser extent in most domains of the economy.

Keep in mind there are still other ways of carrying out segmentation, as the choice depends on the kind of company it is being used on. For example, segmentation based on the size and weight of customers would be useful in the ready-to-wear clothing sector, while segmentation by age would be better for the leisure sector.

Step 2: Communication with the customer

Once the potential clients have been targeted following segmentation, the company will need to come up with a way of communicating with them so that they all feel unique and listened to. This is one of the most important points in customer relationship management, because the number of customers is constantly increasing and they are becoming more and more demanding. The strategy to build the client relationship therefore involves offering and using as many means of communication as possible so that the customer can contact the company however they want, whenever they want, for whatever reason (problems, requests for information, purchases or complaints). The main means of communication include:

- the internet, through email, social media, forums, a chat function on the company website and contact forms;
- mobile devices such as tablets and smartphones, through texts or apps;
- face to face, through a salesperson or sales representative;
- mail;
- fax.

COMMUNICATION STRATEGIES

There are four different marketing communication strategies for reaching the customer.

- **Mass marketing** is the most common strategy. It addresses all consumers without differentiating between them.
- **Differentiated marketing** divides customers into several segments and communicates differently with each of them.
- **Concentrated marketing** focuses on small por-

tions of the market.

- **One-to-one marketing** (actually one-to-few marketing in most cases) involves individual, personalised communication with each consumer.

Step 3: Creation of loyalty

When a customer buys a product or service, the company should do everything in its power to encourage them to buy again and become part of the purchase loop. The technique of the personalised offer can be decisive in ensuring the acquisition of a consumer. This proactive approach implicitly seeks to create customer loyalty by focusing on customer satisfaction. Similarly, the company can put in place a system to deal with questions and complaints, an automatic reminder system for former customers who have not made a purchase for a long time, or a loyalty programme which gives customers reductions once they spend a certain amount.

Salespeople have many ways of earning customer loyalty and building customer relationships. Their main tools include:

- the company website, which provides additional information about the entire catalogue of products;
- newsletters, which remind customers of the company logo and allow the organisation to highlight current special offers;
- invitations to shows or exclusive sales events, in order to create direct contact with the customer and gather their

contact details;
- public relations;
- personalised offers or coupons;
- free samples;
- contact by phone;
- loyalty cards;
- support or after-sales service.

CRM software is by far the most effective tool, as it combines several of the tools from this list.

It is important to point out at this stage that way a company communicates also depends on the industry it is a part of and the type of product it sells. A very technical product, such as a 3D printer for particular industries, will require face-to-face communication as the specific features of the product could be difficult to explain and apply. On the other hand, a more mundane produce can easily be sold over the internet with no need for an intermediary or advisor.

RECOMMENDATIONS

- Make sure that you keep your record of customer details up to date so that you can contact them at any time. Before you apply any of the methods of CRM, check the quality and correctness of your database (watch out for duplication and data entry errors).
- You also need to ensure that your clients' personal data is kept safe, as the company must respect the rights of its customers. These include in particular the right to access, modify and delete their data. Moreover, the company cannot share this data without the client's explicit

consent.

- Do not segment your customers too much, because the groups you define must remain operational (meaning that they can be used by the company). As a reminder, the segments must be homogenous, reachable and different from one another.
- Do not forget to measure the effort invested in your CRM strategy, based on the data you have at your disposal.
- Opt for multichannel communication – and avoid favouring one form in particular – so that customers can choose how they want to contact your company.
- Take a gentle approach to winning over your customers. In other words, do not follow them too closely or you will risk losing them. Remember that it is cheaper to create customer loyalty than to acquire new customers.

CASE STUDY

Example 1: Mobile Telecom, descriptive segmentation

Our first example concerns Mobile Telecom, a telecommunications company which wants to increase its revenue by gaining the loyalty of its existing customers. To do this, it offers phone packages adapted to their usage. After collecting behavioural data on its target group, the marketing team is able to create the summary table below:

Customer	Number of texts	Number of calls
A	15	150
B	85	92
C	23	12
D	157	14
E	145	152
F	65	89
G	18	155
H	150	24
I	15	18
J	154	143

This table compares the number of calls made and texts sent by customers (A to J) over a period of one month. For more visual readers, here is the same information presented as a graph: it reveals clusters of points which form categories of customers.

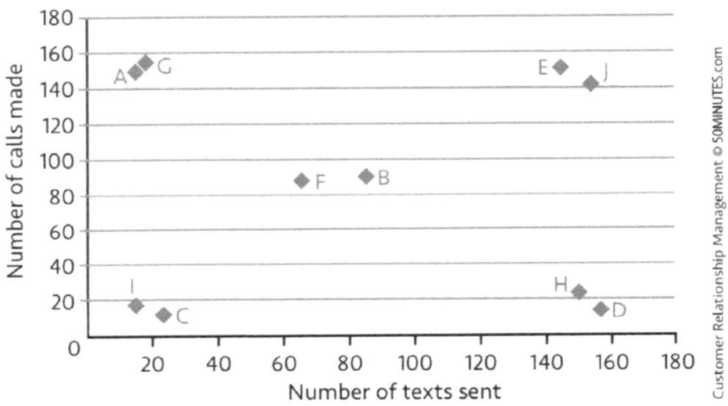

Communication by customer

Looking at it this way, it becomes easy to distinguish between the different customer profiles and divide them into segments. Some use very few texts and calls, others use a bit of both or just one of the two, and the final group uses a lot of both. The company's communication and offers will therefore differ significantly depending on the type of customer.

- **Customers C and I** use very few texts and calls. With this kind of person, marketers may decide to:
  - do everything in their power to move them up into a higher category;
  - ignore them (this is what most often happens) because there is little chance that they will generate a profit for the company one day.
- **Customers B and F** are part of the largest group of consumers. These "average" customers do not have

usage preferences and generate stable revenue. The salespeople's objective is to retain them as customers by occasionally proposing special offers to lead them to become like customers E and J.

- **Customers D/H and A/G** use either mainly texts or mainly calls, no doubt as a matter of preference. It is therefore a good idea to suggest a limited offer, combining for example their preferred type of usage with the other at a better price. This strategy allows the company to broaden the range of products sold and convert some of these customers into very good consumers.
- **Customers E and J** are the best customers. They must be retained at all costs so that they do not go over to the competition. This can be done by giving them increasingly advantageous and personalised special offers: preferential tariffs, a points system based on usage that gives access to other advantages, and so on.

While this graph shows the different categories and strategies to consider for each segment clearly, the reality is often not so simple. Customers may be scattered across the graph, and in this case it will be necessary to carry out more advanced segmentation in order to classify them in a particular group. Finally, in our case many different channels can be used. Phone and texts can be used to reach existing customers, while advertising in the media or through public relations are widely used for more extensive prospecting.

Although it is not always possible to accurately measure the impact of marketing campaigns on sales, some channels, such as direct mailing campaigns, can allow you to monitor the impact of the campaign, or at least get a good estimate.

In this way, the **conversion rate** – from occasional customers to good customers – can be calculated:

$$\text{Conversion rate} = \frac{(\text{Number of customers who have moved into a higher category})}{(\text{Total number of customers})} \times 100$$

If 6 out of 10 of our customers have moved up to a higher offer or increased their consumption, our conversion rate is:

$$\frac{6}{10} \times 100 = 60\,\%$$

It is also possible to calculate the **retention rate** of customers, meaning the percentage of customers who have remained loyal to the company in relation to those who have moved over to the competition. For a full year, the rate is calculated as follows:

$$\text{Retention rate} \; = \; \frac{\text{(Number of customers present for one year or more)}}{\text{(Number of customers present one year ago)}} \times 100$$

If Mobile Telecom had 12 customers last year and eight of them have remained loyal, our retention rate is:

$$\frac{8}{12} \times 100 = 67\,\%$$

Conversely, since the **attrition rate** represents the proportion of the customer base that the company has lost, it can be calculated as follows:

$$\text{Attrition rate} \; = 100\,\% - \text{retention rate}$$

In this case, it is therefore:

$$100\,\% - 67\,\% = 33\,\%$$

Example 2: Home-DIY: a priori/post hoc segmentation

The company in our second case study is Home-DIY, a DIY shop which would like to know and understand its current customers in order to attract others of the same kind who may not be familiar with the company. Unlike with Mobile Telecom, the aim here is not to create customer loyalty, but to look for new prospects.

In order to keep costs as low as possible while ensuring that the procedure remains effective, the manager asks the salespeople to record the postcode of every customer who makes a purchase. In this way, they are able to mark out the current catchment area.

Current catchment area

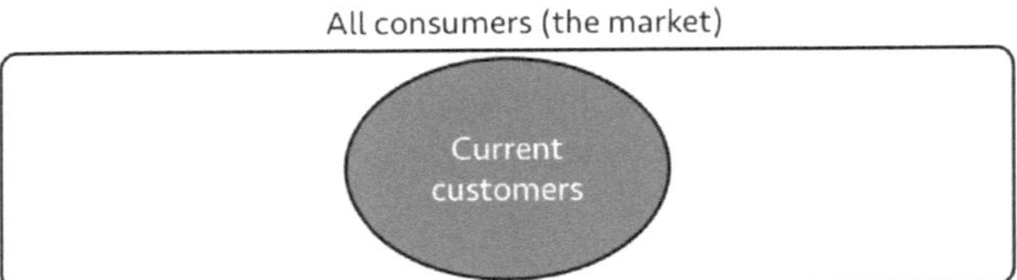

Customer Relationship Management © 50MINUTES.com

After reflecting some more, they define a new theoretical catchment area. This is known as a priori segmentation. Based on where its current customers come from, Home-DIY determines its target market. This is the yellow region which comprises the customers that the company could potentially reach.

A priori segmentation

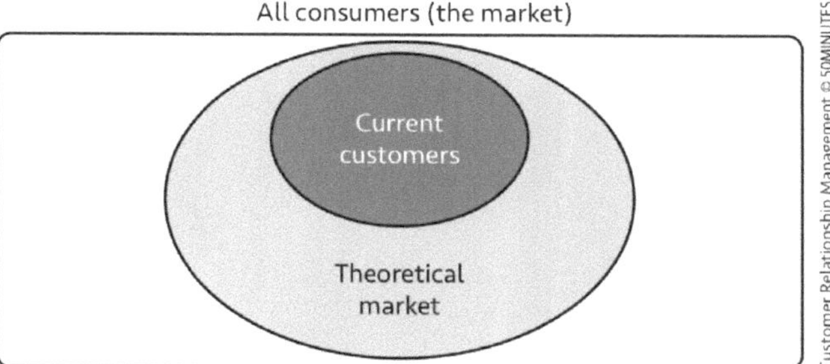

It is now time for a new cycle of segmentation. This is known as post hoc segmentation. Now that it knows the theoretical market, meaning the potential customers in the yellow zone above, the company can address them, for example through an advertising campaign. The new customers who respond favourably will therefore represent the company's real market. This will not necessarily match up with the theoretical market calculated previously:

Post hoc segmentation

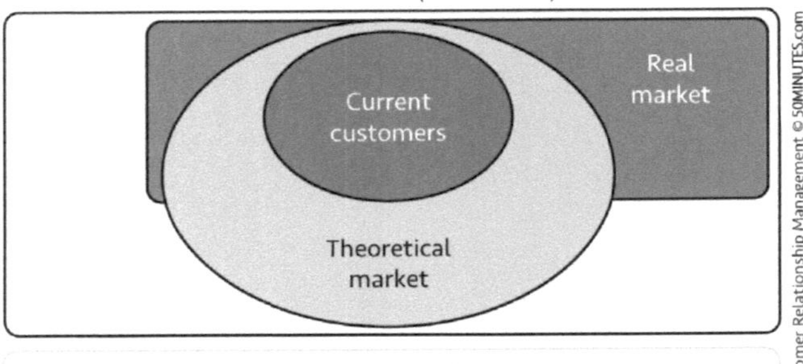

The main marketing efforts are focused on the zone in retrospect

Through a further two-part segmentation, a company can make sure that it only communicates personally with its potential customers. As with the first example, it is recommended to thoroughly check the performance of the new segmentation and the targeting, for example by calculating and drawing conclusions from the conversion rate.

LIMITATIONS AND EXTENSIONS

LIMITATIONS AND CRITICISMS

Although the implementation of a CRM strategy has undeniable benefits for the company, there are nonetheless some limitations to this approach:

- **Personal data**. Companies that apply a CRM approach cannot use customer data however they want. Data handling is governed by a number of regulations, including the European directive dated 24 October 1995 on the protection of personal data. To put it simply, a company cannot gather all types of data, must not use data without the consent of its customers, and must make sure that the data they record can be freely accessed and deleted.

OPT-IN AND OPT-OUT

The concepts of opt-in and opt-out are closely linked to the protection of personal data and are used to define how companies collect data.

- In an opt-in system, the customer gives their explicit prior consent. This means that the internet user ticks (or unticks, in the case of passive opt-in) a box on a form to allow their data to be used for commercial purposes.
- Opt-out systems are an implicit approach. The internet user ticks (or unticks, in the case of passive opt-out) a box on a form to prevent their personal

data from being used. In this case, it is assumed that consent is given until it is withdrawn.

- **Obtaining data**. Related to the first point, acquiring and maintaining customer data can sometimes be a challenge. Large companies can easily access general information such as the customer's name, address and VAT number, but data such as buying preferences is harder to obtain.
- **Identifying customers**. It is sometimes difficult to set up a CRM strategy if customers are hard or impossible to identify. This is the case, for example, for customers passing through a service station: there are a lot of them and they are very varied.
- **Cost**. Implementing and managing a CRM strategy can be relatively costly, especially if it is linked to a broader ERP or if it offers advanced statistical and reporting possibilities.
- **Involving all members of the company in the CRM project**. Sellers and marketers will participate in the project if they see a direct advantage to it (performance improvement, for example). On the other hand, if they just see it as more work, they will not fully commit to it, and the project may end up costing more than it will earn for the company.

RELATED MODELS AND EXTENSIONS

Supplier relationship management (SRM)

Like CRM, SRM is a strategy which allows the company to optimise its relationships with stakeholders – in this case, suppliers. Among other benefits, SRM facilitates communication (often through automated IT programmes), the acquisition of merchandise (this can be done automatically by triggering specific alerts) and the choice, selection and negotiation with suppliers.

Employee relationship management (ERM)

ERM is similar to CRM in that it enables the management of a company's human resources, including salary management, IT access, career supervision, training offers and general communication.

Social CRM

Social CRM is an extension of CRM which works on popular social networks such as Facebook, LinkedIn and Twitter. By offering a further dimension to traditional CRM, the company can gain a better understanding of its customers' desires and consequently respond optimally to their needs.

Vendor relationship management (VRM)

At present, the concept of VRM remains largely theoretical. It emerged at the instigation of consumer associations and aims to allow customers to choose and manage the companies they deal with themselves. Like companies which have

a CRM system with a list of customers, prospects and customers they have lost, the customer will have a list of shops
they currently go to and others which may interest them.
This allows them to manage their information, particularly
their personal data, themselves.

SUMMARY

- Customer relationship management (CRM) refers to all the tools and techniques that allow companies to manage and enrich their relationships with current and former customers and prospects.
- CRM software allows companies to manage a large number of customers – and their data – while addressing them personally.
- CRM adds value to the customer relationship through a range of actions:
  - The segmentation of customers into small, homogenous groups, which allows companies to understand them better and adapt the way they communicate with them. The most commonly used variables are geographical, firmographic, demographic, behavioural, socioeconomic and psychographic.
  - Acquiring the loyalty of existing customers. Since it is easier to obtain the loyalty of current customers than to win over new ones, it is in companies' best interests to implement a CRM strategy (purchase loop).
  - Data reporting, meaning the calculation and analysis of a number of key performance indicators (KPIs), which provide correlations and other statistics to encourage better management of the company together with optimal decision-making (minimisation of risks).
- CRM has significant advantages. By making it easier to manage a large number of customers – which implies preferential and personalised contact with each of them – CRM helps companies to improve the quality of

their service and external communication, which leads to an increase in the net profit per customer and a higher turnover.

- However, the model has its limitations. Companies cannot use all their customers' personal data however they want: they must follow a number of rules to protect customers and their information. It is not always possible to identify customers, which also holds back CRM. Furthermore, the approach can sometimes be very expensive to implement and maintain. Finally, it can be challenging to obtain data such as purchasing preferences.
- Enterprise resource planning (ERP) is linked to CRM and can be used to centralise all the important functions of a company in an application with a unique database. ERM is used to manage human resources and SRM is used to manage suppliers.

We want to hear from you!
Leave a comment on your online library
and share your favourite books on social media!

FURTHER READING

BIBLIOGRAPHY

- Adary, A. (2008) *Évaluez vos actions de communication*. Paris: Éditions Dunod.
- Alard, P. (2000) *La stratégie de relation client*. Paris: Éditions Dunod.
- Amidou, L. (2012) *Marketing des réseaux sociaux*. Boulogne-Billancourt: MA Éditions.
- Bennett, T. (2014) 7 Types of Market Segmentation. *Udemy Blog*. [Online]. [Accessed 14 July 2017]. Available from: <https://blog.udemy.com/types-of-market-segmentation/>
- C-Radar. (No date) *La firmographie : un outil intelligent pour comprendre, identifier, vérifier et détecter*. [Online]. [Accessed 14 July 2017]. Available from: <https://www.c-radar.com/blog/2014/09/19/firmographie-outil-intelligent-comprendre-identifier-verifier-detecter/>
- Delers, A. (2014) *Le principe de Pareto*. Namur: Éditions Lemaitre Publishing.
- Van Dessel, G. (No date) Net Promotor Score – calcul et application. *CheckMarket*. [Online]. [Accessed 14 July 2017]. Available from: <https://fr.checkmarket.com/blog/votre-net-promoter-score/>
- Divard, R. (2010) *Le marketing participatif*. Paris: Éditions Dunod.
- Ghannam-Zaim, O. (2012) La Segmentation. *Institut Supérieur du Commerce et d'Administrations des entreprises*. [Online]. [Accessed 14 July 2017]. Available from: <https://fr.slideshare.net/enams90/

la-segmentation-en-marketing>
- Project VRM. (No date) Main Page. *Cyber Law Harvard.* [Online]. [Accessed 14 July 2017]. Available from: <https://cyber.harvard.edu/projectvrm/Main_Page>
- Krebs, G. (2004) *Nouvelles pratiques client-fournisseur.* Saint-Denis-La-Plaine: Afnor.
- Lefébure, R. and Venturi, G. (2004) *Gestion de la relation client.* Paris: Éditions Eyrolles.
- McMahon, C. (No date) The 16 Marketing KPIs You Should Be Measuring (But Probably Aren't). *VLT Design.* [Online]. [Accessed 14 July 2017]. Available from: <https://vtldesign.com/digital-marketing/16-marketing-kpis-to-measure/>
- Peelen, E., Jallat, F. and Stevens, É. (2014) *Gestion de la relation client. Total relationship management, Big data and marketing mobile.* Paris: Pearson.
- Rao, S. S. (1998) Diaper-beer syndrome. *Forbes.* [Online]. [Accessed 14 July 2017]. Available from: <https://www.forbes.com/forbes/1998/0406/6107128a.html>
- Rouse, M. (2014) Customer Relationship Management. *TechTarget.* [Online]. [Accessed 14 July 2017]. Available from: <http://searchcrm.techtarget.com/definition/CRM>

ADDITIONAL SOURCES

- Brown, M. S. (2014) *Data Mining for Dummies.* Hoboken, New Jersey: John Wiley & Sons, Inc.
- Buttle, F. (2015) *Customer Relationship Management: Concept and Technologies.* Abingdon: Routledge.
- Kumar, V. and Reinartz, W. (2012) *Customer Relationship*

Management: Concept, Strategy, and Tools. Second edition. New York: Springer.

- Payne, A. (2005) *Handbook of CRM: Achieving Excellence Through Customer Management*. London: Routledge.
- Peelen, E. and Beltman, R. (2013) *Customer Relationship Management*. Cambridge: Pearson.
- Pennington, A. (2016) *The Customer Experience Book: How to Design, Measure and Improve Customer Experience in Your Business*. Cambridge: Pearson.
- Watkinson, M. (2012) *The Ten Principles Behind Great Customer Experiences*. Cambridge: Pearson.